BACK TO SCHOOL

A Global Journey

Maya Ajmera • John D. Ivanko

Answering a question in the United States

In support of
global fund for children

🪷 Charlesbridge

Going to school means learning about the world around you.

Reading together in the Amazon rain forest in Brazil

Planting trees in Mexico to help the environment

Sharing a desk with a classmate in Côte d'Ivoire

There are many kinds of schools . . .

Taking homeschool classes over the radio in the Australian Outback

Learning in a bright and colorful classroom in Cuba

Attending night school in India

and lots of ways to get to them.

Walking with friends in Mauritius

Riding a camel in Mongolia

Biking in the United States

Taking a boat in Myanmar

You might go to school in a uniform

Attending school under the trees in Ghana

Giggling with classmates in Tanzania

Hanging out with a friend between classes in India

or wear your favorite outfit.

Walking home together in Kyrgyzstan

Going to school means learning from teachers, classmates, books, and computers.

Learning to write in Ecuador

Sharing a computer in China

You learn to read and write and count and calculate.

Forming words on a slate in Bangladesh

Doing long-division math in Jordan

Reading independently in South Africa

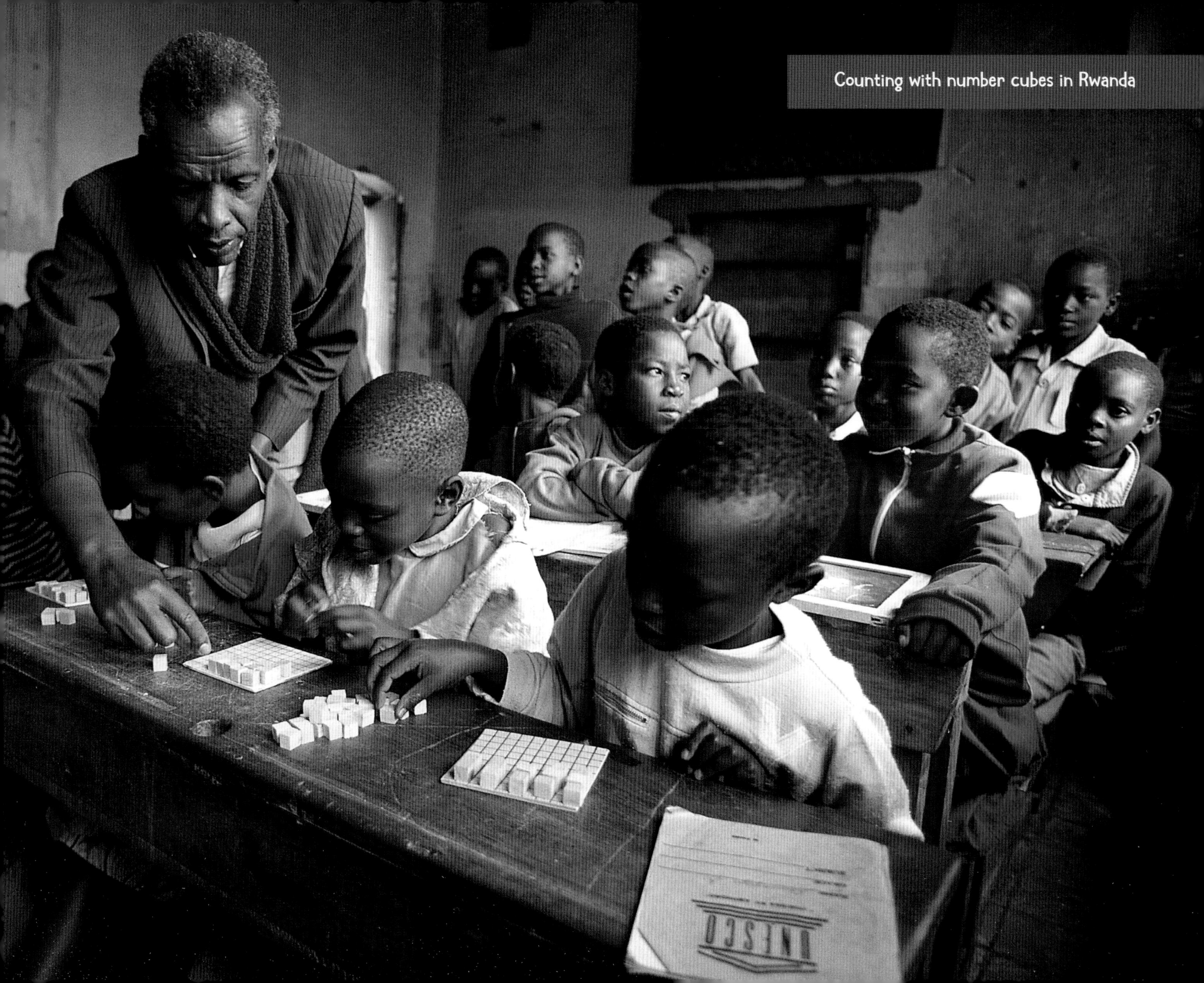

Counting with number cubes in Rwanda

Discovering how motors and electricity work in Ghana

You build things and conduct experiments to understand how the world works.

Mixing liquids in chemistry class in Germany

Looking into a microscope in the United States

You discover different languages.

Learning Mandarin Chinese in the United States

Practicing sign language in South Africa

Studying a second language in France

You might even learn to code on a computer.

Using a computer in Cameroon

You develop your artistic and musical talents.

Drawing a picture in Bhutan

Learning about aerial photography in Suriname

Singing in a chorus in the United States

Going to school means exploring new places and experiencing new things.

Touching a plasma ball at a science museum in the Netherlands

Handling sea creatures in Iceland

Visiting with a potter in Thailand

Touching a baby elephant in Kenya

You go on field trips
and join sports teams
and clubs.

Competing in a chess tournament in Russia

Encouraging a soccer teammate in Japan

Making waves with a parachute during gym class in the United States

You exercise and play with your friends.

Playing soccer before school in Ecuador

Going down the slide at recess in Japan

You learn how to be a good citizen in your community, nation, and world.

Cleaning up the beach in New Zealand

Working together to move a log in Vietnam

Going to school means working hard, having fun, and making lifelong friends!

Studying with friends on a hillside in Nepal

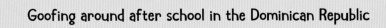

Goofing around after school in the Dominican Republic

Where You Learn

No two schools are the same. Some schools have many rooms and are full of computers, books, maps, and art supplies. Others have just one room, and some hold classes outside. Some schools are just for boys or just for girls, and some are for boys and girls together. Whether large or small, in your home or far away, school is one of the best places to explore new ideas.

How You Learn

There are lots of ways to learn. Every school day brings new experiments, stories, songs, and problems to solve. You do some assignments on your own and work on others with your classmates. You might use paper, a slate, a chalkboard, or a computer. You go on field trips to see things up close. Schools around the world teach reading, writing, math, science, and history. In many schools, music and art classes help you develop your creativity. All these experiences help you discover which subjects you like most and encourage you to think about what you want to be when you grow up.

Reading a big book together in Australia

Kids go to school everywhere.

Iceland

Netherlands

Germany

France

Canada

United States

Mexico

Cuba

Dominican Republic

Guatemala

Suriname

Côte d'Ivoire

Ghana

Ecuador

Camero

Brazil

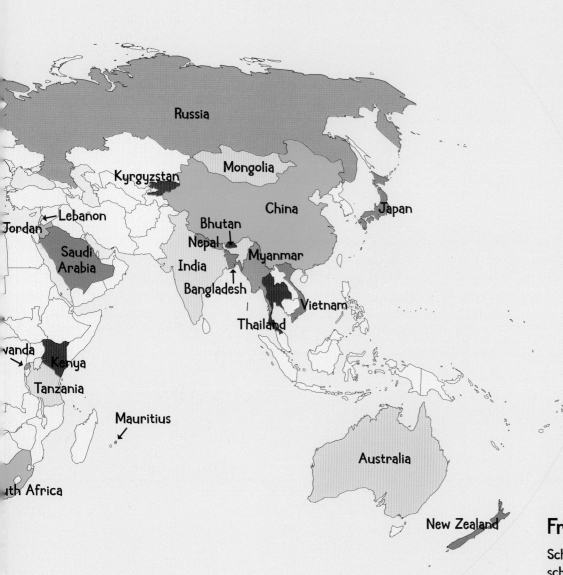

Russia

Kyrgyzstan

Mongolia

China

Japan

Bhutan

Nepal

Myanmar

Lebanon

Jordan

Saudi
Arabia

India

Bangladesh

Vietnam

Thailand

wanda

Kenya

Tanzania

th Africa

Mauritius

Australia

New Zealand

Using a tablet computer during class in Canada

Who Teaches You?

Your teachers guide you and help you solve difficult problems. They want you to succeed and to be your best. Your family and friends can also help you learn. Sometimes they tutor you or help you with your homework. They also offer encouragement as you take on new challenges.

Being a Good Student

Knowing the answer to a tough question feels great. Getting there involves hard work and commitment. Writing well, counting correctly, and remembering important people and places are things you have to do on your own. School is also a place to learn how to be a good citizen and help others in your community. Going to school is a big step toward growing up and learning to be responsible.

Friendship and Fun

School is a great place to make friends and have fun. Through after-school activities you can meet other kids who share your interests. Hanging out with friends, playing tag at recess, and working with other students on a class project can be some of the best things about school.

To Talia, who is passionate about learning, making, and exploring—M. A.

To Liam Kivirist, who has, as a homeschooler, embraced lifelong learning and cultivated a curiosity, especially with technology, that would make any teacher proud—J. D. I.

Maya Ajmera thanks Adele Richardson Ray for her wonderful support of *Back to School*.

Text copyright © 2019 by Maya Ajmera and John D. Ivanko
Photographs copyright © by individual copyright holders
All rights reserved, including the right of reproduction in whole or in part in any form.
Charlesbridge and colophon are registered trademarks of Charlesbridge Publishing, Inc.

At the time of publication, any URLs printed in this book were accurate and active. Charlesbridge and the authors are not responsible for the content or accessibility of any URL.

Published by Charlesbridge
85 Main Street
Watertown, MA 02472
(617) 926-0329
www.charlesbridge.com

Library of Congress Cataloging-in-Publication Data
Names: Ajmera, Maya, author. | Ivanko, John D. (John Duane), 1966– author.
Title: Back to school: a global journey / Maya Ajmera, John D. Ivanko.
Description: Revised Edition. | Watertown, Massachusetts: Charlesbridge, [2019]
Identifiers: LCCN 2017012707 | ISBN 9781580898379 (reinforced for library use) | ISBN 9781580898409 (softcover) | ISBN 9781632897763 (ebook) | ISBN 9781632897770 (ebook pdf)
Subjects: LCSH: Education, Elementary—Juvenile literature. | Elementary schools—Juvenile literature.
Classification: LCC LB1556 .A56 2019 | DDC 372—dc23
LC record available at https://lccn.loc.gov/2017012707

Printed in Malaysia
(hc) 10 9 8 7 6 5 4 3 2 1
(sc) 10 9 8 7 6 5 4 3 2 1

Display type set in Canvas Text Sans by Yellow Design Studio
Text type set in Digby by Atlantic Fonts
Color separations by Colourscan Print Co Pte Ltd, Singapore
Printed by TWP Sdn Bhd in Johor Bahru, Johor, Malaysia
Production supervision by Brian G. Walker
Designed by Susan Mallory Sherman

Writing on the chalkboard in Saudi Arabia

Photo Credits: FRONT COVER: © Werli Francois/Alamy Stock Photo. BACK COVER: © Stuart Fox/Gallo Images/age fotostock. TITLE PAGE: p. 1: © Blend Images/Alamy Stock Photo. LEARNING ABOUT THE WORLD: p. 2: © Ton Koene/age fotostock. p. 3: © Environmental Images/Universal Images Group/age fotostock. MANY KINDS OF SCHOOLS: p. 4: © Danita Delimont/Alamy Stock Photo. p. 5: left, © Grant Rooney/age fotostock; top right, © Patrick Ward/Alamy Stock Photo; bottom right, © Monkmeyer/Sidney. LOTS OF WAYS TO GET TO THEM: p. 6: left, © FB-StockPhoto-1/Alamy Stock Photo; top right, © Roger Arnold/Alamy Stock Photo; bottom right, © Dasha Rosato/Alamy Stock Photo. p. 7: © Charles O. Cecil/age fotostock. UNIFORM OR FAVORITE OUTFIT: p. 8: top left, © A. Kauffeld/USAID/Wikimedia Commons/File:Ghana school under the trees.jpg/public domain; bottom left, © Ton Koene/age fotostock; right, © Vivek Manek/Dinodia Photo/age fotostock. p. 9: © Thornton Cohen/Alamy Stock Photo. LEARNING FROM TEACHERS: p. 10: © Rolf Schulten/imageBROKER/age fotostock. p. 11: © BEIJING BEAUTY VIEW P/View Stock/age fotostock. READING, WRITING, COUNTING: p. 12: top left, © 2000 Jon Warren; bottom left, © Greatstock/Alamy Stock Photo; right, © Ton Koene/age fotostock. p. 13: © Betty Press/Woodfin Camp. BUILDING THINGS AND CONDUCTING EXPERIMENTS: p. 14: © Olivier Asselin/Alamy Stock Photo. p. 15: left, © MITO images GmbH/Alamy Stock Photo; right, © Richard Nowitz. DIFFERENT LANGUAGES: p. 16: top left, © Stefanie Felix/The Image Works; bottom left, © Godong/Universal Images Group/age fotostock; right, © Elaine Little. p. 17: © imageBROKER/Alamy Stock Photo. ARTISTIC AND MUSICAL TALENTS: p. 18: left, © 2000 Jon Warren; right, © frans lemmens/Alamy Stock Photo. p. 19: © Jeff Greenberg/age fotostock. EXPLORING NEW PLACES: p. 20: left, © Tom Ferguson/Alamy Stock Photo; right, © Ragnar Th. Sigurdsson/age fotostock. p. 21: © pavlos christoforou/Alamy Stock Photo. FIELD TRIPS, SPORTS TEAMS, CLUBS: p. 22: © Peter Langer/Axiom Photographic/age fotostock. p. 23: left, © Andrew Catta/Alamy Stock Photo; right, © AFLO/Aflo Foto Agency Royalty Free/age fotostock. EXERCISE AND PLAY: p. 24: Scott Keeler/Tampa Bay Times/ZUMA Press/Alamy Stock Photo. p. 25: left, © imageBROKER/Alamy Stock Photo; right, © Malcolm Fairman/Alamy Stock Photo. BEING A GOOD CITIZEN: p. 26: left, © chameleonseye/Essentials Collection/iStock; right, © Stephen Ford/Alamy Stock Photo. p. 27: © Dennis Cox/Alamy Stock Photo. WORKING HARD, HAVING FUN, MAKING FRIENDS: p. 28: © 2000 Jon Warren. p. 29: © Monkmeyer/Bopp. KIDS GO TO SCHOOL EVERYWHERE: p. 30: © Bill Bachman/Alamy Stock Photo. p. 31: © FatCamera/Signature Collection/iStock. COPYRIGHT PAGE: p. 32: © Katrina Thomas/Aramco World.

Photo Research: Julie Alissi/J8 Media